For SOLANNE c.m.

Many thanks to the staff and children at
Chalvey Nursery School and Assessment Unit,
and Salt Hill Nursery for their help and advice.

Copyright © 1996 De Agostini Editions Ltd
Illustrations copyright © 1996 Clare Mackie

All rights reserved.

Edited by Anna McQuinn
Designed by Sarah Godwin and Suzy McGrath

First published in the United States in 1996 by
De Agostini Editions Ltd, 919 Third Avenue, New York, N Y 10022

Distributed by Stewart, Tabori & Chang,
a division of U.S. Media Holdings, Inc., New York, N Y

ISBN 1-899883-42-8
Library in Congress Catalog Card Number: 96-83069

Printed and bound in Italy

There are
lots of things
to count on every
page - make sure
you don't miss
them.

Crazy Creatures
Counting

Written by **Hannah Reidy**

Illustrated by **Clare Mackie**

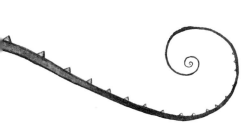

One

dippy,
dopey
creature -
wondering
about
a one.

Two
toothless,
tip-toeing
creatures -
timidly
touching
a two.

Three

**careful,
calculating
creatures -
seriously
studying
a three.**

Four

fabulous,
flashy
creatures -
dizzily
dancing
with
a four.

Five
heavy,
hairy
creatures -
happily
hugging
a five.

Six
silly, skinny
creatures -
pinkily
kissing
a six.

Seven

swooshing
and
whooshing
creatures -
hustling,
bustling and
skiing down
a seven.

Eight

late, putting-
on-weight
creatures -
lunching,
by munching
and crunching
an eight.

Nine

nice but
naughty
creatures -
slipping and
slopping,
dripping and
dropping
their paint on
a nine.